I've Been Thinking

Don Bell

Kristi
Nice to have you
in the w'shop
9/9/93 *Don*

Aouse of the **9** Muses, Inc.

Palm Beach, Florida

Cover designed by Ann Francis.
Illustrations by Jack Mastrofski

For additional information and for discount schedules on bulk purchases, contact the publishers:

House of the 9 Muses, Inc.
Box 2974
Palm Beach, Florida 33480

Library of Congress Cataloging-in-Publication Data

Bell, Don, 1927-
    I've been thinking / by Don Bell.
        p.   cm.
    ISBN 1-56412-000-7 (pbk.) : $8.95
    1. Conduct of life--Anecdotes. 2.Interpersonal communication--Anecdotes. 3. Des Moines (Iowa)-- Anecdotes. 4. Bell, Don, 1927-
--Anecdotes.   I. Title. II. Title: I have been thinking.
BF637.C5B45   1991
158--dc20   91-17223
                                                   CIP

Printed in the United States of America

Introduction

Why would you be interested in what I've been thinking? For the same reasons that all of us like to listen in on the thoughts of other people: It's encouraging to hear that they often think the same way we do; and it's enlightening to get their slightly different perspectives to help us understand and cope with human nature - our own and the nature of people we love, work with or serve.

Most of these pieces were written for a Des Moines paper, The Skywalker. I have chosen thirty that I feel are the most encouraging and enlightening from the fifty that were published and, in some cases, I have added afterthoughts to reflect how my ideas about things - or the things themselves - have changed over the past few years.

I hope that some of the true stories you find here will give you ideas for your personal growth and for your enjoyment of yourself and other people. I hope that the rest will, at the very least, be uplifting and entertaining.

Don Bell
Management Management, Inc.
2413 - 81 Circle • Des Moines, Iowa 50322
515 253-0834

Contents

Be A Go-Giver

She walked briskly toward me, with hand extended. "Congratulations, Don!" she said. "You did a fine job."

"Thanks," I stammered, far from my usual loquacious self. I had no idea who she was, but congratulations are always welcome.

We were at the luxurious new Hyatt Regency in Washington, D.C., attending the 1987 annual convention of the International Platform Association. Our days and nights had been filled with presentations from the likes of Ted Turner, Secretary of Defense Casper Weinberger, Sam Donaldson, Mrs. Lowell Thomas, Jack Anderson and Malcolm Forbes.

In the midst of all this, there had been an international public speaking contest. After withstanding four days of eliminations, I emerged third. Thus the kind words from the gracious lady who introduced herself as Myrna.

"How does it feel, now that it's over?" she asked.

"Well, O.K., I guess," I answered. "I am a little disappointed..."

"Disappointed." she repeated, raising her eyebrows. "How could you be disappointed with being third in that group of speakers? What possible difference will it make in your life if you're first or fifth among the five finalists?"

A cozy bar only thirty feet away beckoned. I was tired and thirsty, and Myrna talked about

1

such interesting things. "Will you join me for a drink?" I asked.

"No," she countered, "I must get cleaned up for dinner. But tell me, how will you use this experience?"

"Use it? Why, gosh, I don't know..." The ludicrous thought crossed my mind that I teach goal setting , yet was unable to articulate my own goals. But why should this stranger care? "Get cleaned up"? - she was immaculate. She was also tall, athletic and dressed in a stylish daytime suit with complementary jewelry. And she didn't waste time in idle conversation while I played detective.

"Look," she said, "I will have that drink. You need a little help."

Over a Seven-Up she was completely at ease with herself and with me. She quickly pointed out my strengths and gave me ideas for my career that were stimulating. It seemed that she knew more about me from hearing my ten-minute speech than I knew about myself.

"What do you do?" I finally had occasion to ask.

"I'm in the Army," she said casually.

"And what do you do in the Army?" I pressed.

"I'm in personnel," she answered , impatient to get back to ideas for my future. Moments later she glanced at her watch and rose to leave with, "Sorry, but I must go. Here's my card. Good luck to you, Don."

I pocketed her card without a glance and watched her disappear up the escalator. "She'll go far with the Army," I predicted. "She's intelligent and personable, with an uncanny understanding of human behavior."

I took a closer look at her card, then sat down to finish my drink.

It's interesting, isn't it: Real leaders have no need to flaunt their titles or hide behind trappings of office. They live and lead as go-givers, not go-getters, and it is the giving that shapes and strengthens their character. Myrna showed me that being Number One or Number Three is not as important as following through with a plan to be of service.

That's why she is Number One:
> Myrna Williamson, Brigadier General
> U.S. Army
> Commanding General,
> U.S. Army Third ROTC Region,
> Fort Riley, Kansas.

After Thought

Myrna retired from the Army in 1989. I was invited to a party in her honor in Washington, DC., but could not attend. A popular magazine recently featured her in a nice article.

A classy lady.

This Is A Recording...

The package was from California. The handwritten address confirmed my suspicion that the contents was a Father's Day present from my children. With trembling hands (I confess: I'm still a child at heart) I ripped away at the packing to discover a black box calling itself a "Record a Call - One Button AutoCommand System." Euphemisms aside, my children banned together to push me deeper into the Electronic Age with a telephone answering machine.

I love them for it, or to be precise, I love them for themselves and I appreciate their remembrances. But I'm not sure I'm ready for a one button autocommand system. It's not that I'm not into electronics: this is being written on my computer/word processor which has all the electronic whistles and bells. But these answering machines seem so impersonal. It somehow seems like a breach of faith for one who touts open and dynamic two-way communication to let a machine tell you what you just figured out on your own: I am unable to answer your call at this time. There are two strategically placed phones in this compact tenth-floor condo, and if I haven't answered after six rings you know that I am unable.

But after only two days I have mellowed. I came home today, pushed the button, and heard a lovely voice tell me that it's nice that I've "gone modern" as she'd been trying to reach me for a week and had all but given up. Wow. That was close.

I called the kids at their three separate residences to thank them, and you know what I'm going to tell you: I reached their three answering machines. What a world.

And will you believe this? My machine has been talking with another machine. The other unit lacked the good grace to hear out my greeting, so most of its message was lost, but I think my order is in at Sears.

So perhaps I have been wrong. Even cold, impersonal mechanical communication is better than no communication. And if a machine can help keep us in touch, then I'm all for it. I'm sure I'll hear from a lot of folks who have selected me to receive a one-year free subscription, and every would-be president will leave a message asking for my support, but that's all part of it.

So when you call me, you may get my one button autocommand system, but I promise that I won't tell you that I am unable, etc. And I won't belabor you with instructions to leave your name, the time of your call, your phone number and a message of any length. If you don't know that by now, where have you been? You know I'll return your call, and sooner or later, machine or no machine, we'll talk with each other. I look forward to it.

After Thought

Almost three years and 30,000 phone calls later and I still have the "one button auto-command system." I could write a book about the calls it has taken. When Jane and I were married early this year, it moved with me from my tenth-floor condo into her suburban townhouse where it serves us and Julie, my new teen-age daughter.

It's curious, isn't it, how we seem to adapt to new customs and rituals. I would expect that, with the exception of pre-teens learning to use the phone, most people have reached and talked to dozens, or hundreds, of answering machines. The novelty has long since passed, but we still feel the need to patiently explain that your chances of ever having a return call from me are slim unless you leave your name, number, time of call, date of birth and a message of any length after, that's AFTER, you hear the beeep.

By the time this book is printed and works its way into your hands, you may have experienced the next generation of machines that a phone company is trying to sell to me. They say it will let me leave a recording just for you if you're not home when I call. Your phone will be dialed up to eight times to deliver my message. I hope you've enjoyed the messages from siding companies, carpet cleaners and worthy causes. I assume they've all left their name, number and time of call along with their message of questionable length.

A Laughing Matter

Have you had a good laugh lately? Not a nervous little twitter, or a silly giggle, but a stomach-clutching, eye-watering, knee-bending guffaw that leaves you gasping for air? You need one a day, I believe, and several would be even better.

Laughing is good for your health, your wealth, and your happiness.

Last week, Des Moines' other paper printed an article that Norman Cousins wrote for Consumers Digest magazine titled, "The body's healing force: The brain." Cousins' point is that our brain produces and combines a variety of secretions which are more effective at fighting disease than the most potent man-made drugs.

Although he didn't mention it in this piece, you may remember that Cousins wrote a book over a decade ago called "Anatomy of an Illness," in which he tells how he used laughter to help his brain release these secretions. His own body, apparently encouraged by laughter, did what medical science thought was close to impossible: It brought him back from near death to good health.

Dr. Jeffrey Goldstein of Temple University, Philadelphia, contends that longevity may very well be related to laughter. He says that tension brings on many of our illnesses, and that laughter is the best way to relieve tension. Most of us can relate to that.

In every speech class or workshop I conduct, I use laughter and humor to reduce tension. I find that laughter settles many queasy stomachs and lets students enjoy what, for some, is a frightening experience.

But you don't have to be deathly ill or even mildly uncomfortable to have laughter improve your health. A hearty laugh provides many of the good effects of jogging with no possible damage to your feet and without the subsequent need for a shower. Laughter increases your pulse rate, gets fresh oxygen into the blood, and gently massages your heart, liver, and kidneys.

Laughter aids digestion, too, and that helps explain why it has been the custom for centuries to bring out the court jester and entertainers following a banquet. When you have been subjected to as much banquet fare as I have, you realize that the digestive system needs all the help it can get.

Having been in or around the field of education most of my life, I know that people learn best when they learn with humor. I feel that you will prosper in your business, and that your business will prosper if you don't take too sober a view of yourself. Oscar Wilde once said that people are never so trivial as when they take themselves seriously.

Several months ago I flew to Detroit to make a presentation. The flight was rough and we were late arriving in Chicago. It took forever to continue because several Chicago runways were closed due to snow, ice, and -- if you would believe some of the other passengers -- piles of crashed jets.

The final leg of the journey proved equal to the first for roller coaster effects, but preparations were finally made to land. The liquor cart -- the source of false hope and the only form of recreation for an astonishing number of people-- was put away. But, alas, we were put into a holding pattern and landing was set back almost an hour.

The delay caused half the passengers to sober up and desperately need another drink. Some of the passengers became bored and desperately needed another drink, and the rest of us became apprehensive that we would miss our appointments.

The "no smoking" light flashed on and the long awaited landing soon followed -- but about ten seconds too soon. It was the hardest bone-crunching touchdown I've ever experienced. Several people screamed, several cursed while others prayed, checked for sprained necks, or checked for their attorneys' phone numbers.

A scant moment later, a flight attendant, in her most cheery voice, announced over the intercom, "For those of you who haven't noticed, we've just landed in Detroit!"

Her line was delivered with just the right touch to make us all laugh and forget our complaints. I don't know if she made it up, or if it was company policy, but that's my kind of airline. Laughter and humor paid off.

Yes, laughter affects your happiness. Don't wait until you are happy to have a good laugh:

Laughter can make you happy. I used to drop in on an old friend who lived alone following the death of his wife.

One night I found him laughing uproariously at some inane TV show. I was almost embarrassed, but he said, "Don, I know it's not all that funny, but I need a really good laugh, and I refuse to let poor material deny me of it."

We both had a good laugh over that, and I went away knowing that my friend was in good shape, and that our friendship was stronger.

Friends, employee groups and families that laugh together, stay together. Laughter defuses emotionally charged situations. I've always felt that people like Bob Hope and Louis Armstrong did more for our country with a laugh and a grin than many of the dour and humorless individuals who represent us.

So put some real laughter into your life. It will make life more pleasant for you and for those around you. It will do wonders for your health, your wealth and your happiness.

After Thought

The executive director for a large account invited me to join the group when Norman Cousins addressed their convention in Des Moines last year. She knows I'm a fan of Dr. Cousins, and you can bet I did not demure.

Cousins was at his best, which is to say he was fantastic. As former editor of Saturday Review, he tells it as he sees it, and he told this convention of healthcare executives that medical doctors are trained in the power of libel law rather than the healing power of positive communication.

He told us that 85% of the people in hospitals are self-regulated, which is to say that the way they think about their sickness contributes to their sickness rather than to their good health. He said that once patients find out what they *have* they get *worse*.

Knowing that we can let our mind talk our body into being sick, the good news is that we can just as easily let it talk the body into getting well. And one of the things that our body responds to is laughter which releases endorphens, because endorphens are good guys who, like Pac Man, eat up the bad guys in our system.

During a public seminar a man said to me that he was a medical doctor, and he couldn't use my ideas about getting ourselves and others to think positively.

"Do you know what would happen if I tell a fella that he stands a good chance of getting well? That good humor and a positive attitude will help his recovery, and then he dies?

"His family will remember that I said he stands a good chance and they'll come after me for every cent I've got. No. Not me. I *have* to tell him he's probably not going to make it!"

Can you imagine ? A doctor trained by a lawyer. I wish he could hear Norman Cousins, or my cheerful young doctor.

I went to him with a cough that wouldn't let me finish one sentence without a hack.

"You got one mean Bronchitis, Don," he

said with a smile. "But you take four of these a day and in five days you'll be back at the podium shaking the chandeliers. Why, this stuff is so good it could put me out of business. I might have to join you on the lecture circuit to make an easy buck."

"Hey," I wheezed, " You work your side of the street and let me work mine."

We had a good laugh, but I wonder where I'd be with the same medicine and a cautious prognosis from the fellow at the seminar?

We Can Be Civil

The party was in full swing when he made his grand entrance. I suspected him of sitting at home, waiting until several dozen of his friends had gathered to give him a rousing welcome. It's an old trick, and, to my slight annoyance, it worked again at this party.

I don't like the man, and who can blame me? He is arrogant, conceited and brash. He talks too loudly and his raucous laugh is a ploy to draw flagging attention back to him. And on the night of this party he was, as usual, overdressed for the occasion.

As he strutted past me, with his beautiful wife hanging on his arm, his eyes looked straight through me, as if I did not exist. Naturally, I stared right back through him. What else could one do?

"One could be civil," a small voice inside me said. Having no smart reply to that, I waited until he came my way again, drew a shallow breath and offered, "Hi. How's it going?"

A slightly raised brow showed that he had not expected this from me, but he managed a weak, "Hangin' in," without breaking stride.

You see? I was right. The cad has no class. But what's this? A half hour later he was back, and talking to me.

15

"Nice party, Don."

"Yeah. Really. Nice party." I didn't expect this from him, either.

"Don, I want you to know how much I enjoy your articles in the Skywalker..."

As he talked, I couldn't help but notice what a rich, full voice this gentleman had. He seemed sure of himself, as intelligent, well-adjusted people are, and his eyes showed that he is deeply interested in other people. I wanted to tell him that it was nice to see a person elegantly dressed for a party, but he was still talking about me, and I was loath to change the subject.

As our conversation wound down, he gracefully moved on to talk with our host. I heard him laugh the zesty laugh of one who enjoys life. What a splendid fellow. I must get to know him better!

I had risked something by opening up to him, but the risk was not as great as it seemed at the time. He, perhaps, risked more by seeking me out. I don't want to make more of this than there is, but I suspect that his feelings toward me were about the same as mine were toward him. By opening up we have each made a new friend, and we won't have to waste a ton of energy disliking one another.

Perhaps there is something in this story for you. Perhaps you can do something about that person in your office who gives you the icy stare every day, or the neighbor who goes out of his way to avoid conversation, or the uncle who never has accepted you as one of the family.

You can be civil, risk yourself with them, and try a little non-controversial conversation. They may not be articulate as my friend at the party, and it may take them longer to realize that you are sincere. And they may be more fearful of rejection by you than my new friend was of me. But hang in. If it takes a week, or a month, or a year, a better relationship will be worth any effort you make.

My Mother Can't Swim

I wish I'd had the time to tell her about my mother not being able to swim, but 18-year-old nieces don't sit still long at family reunions.

She had just shown us her drawings and they were really good. Not just good for a young girl -- good for a mature artist of any age. Her Irish Setter rendition wasn't your generic, art-book Setter; here was a dog that had hunted ducks and who was eager to jump in after one right now.

After showering her with well deserved congratulations, most of the family drifted off and left her with my brother-in-law and me.

"What do you plan to do with your talent?" I asked.

"Do with it," she countered, "Gosh, I don't know. What do you think I should do?"

"If they were mine I'd show them to every ad agency and employer in town," was my easy answer.

"Oh, but I can't talk to employers," she shuddered. "I can't do that."

I was on vacation, and I needed to get away from work, but the teacher in me began to stir.

"You can't talk to employers. You've tried, but it never works out. Employers are a special breed that you hold in awe."

"Well, I don't know about 'awe', Uncle Don," she said, "but I sure can't talk with them."

I asked if the problem was a physical one. She laughed and said no, she was fine physically; and no, her mother had not been scared by an employer; and yes, she admitted to better than average intelligence.

"Then we're left with it being nothing more than something that you think; some idea that's lodged in your mind?"

She tried to laugh at that, but couldn't. "Do I hear you saying that all I need to do is *think* that I can talk to them and I'll be able to?"

"What else? But look," I cautioned, "You've been telling yourself that you can't for a long time. It will take your mind some time to get used to the idea that you can. Keep working at it and your mind is bound to get the message."

"I'll give it a try, thanks. It might just work," and she was off to sample the watermelon.

The story about my mother would have stressed my point, but our moment was over. She seemed to get the idea, and there was no point in beating it to death; but the story is very meaningful to me and has helped me through some dark times.

You see, my mother can't swim. The reason, she would tell you, is that she can't float. She would say this with some pride, as if nature had singled her out from the rest of us with some force that caused her body to sink. Now, I don't mean gently sink: I'm talking about your oft-mentioned rock. Every summer Dad would go through a ritual, hoping that her bones might have become less dense over the long winter. He would wade into the lake, encouraging Mom to follow. He would support her head with one hand and her body with the other, then withdraw the hand holding her body.

As soon as he let go, Mother was upright. "See?" she would say, "I can't float!" She would take off her swim cap, shake out her hair, and retire to a shady spot with a book while the rest of us got our fill of swimming. The ritual was over until the next summer.

When the family moved to Florida, my brother and I took our turn with her from the dock in our back yard. Even in the buoyant salt water the results were the same, and we finally all gave in to it: Mother can't float.

Many years later, however, when mother was on the up side of 50, grandma -- mother's mother -- was standing on the dock taking the sun, when the wind caught her scarf and blew it into the bay just out of reach. But grandma reached.

Either mother heard the splash, or some maternal instinct drew her from the house. Dad saw the rest as she dashed bayward from the front yard. Mother eased herself into the six-foot-deep water, took two powerful strokes out, and five flailing strokes back with grandma in tow. The three reached the dock at the same instant, and Dad hauled in the two women. It was not much of a swim, but for one who sinks like a rock it might as well have been the English Channel.

Unfortunately for mother, it was too late. Oh, they survived the swim; grandma for 15 years; mother is holding up well at 86; but mother felt that is was too late in life to profit from the knowledge that she could, indeed, both float and swim. I often wish that grandma had chased the scarf 30 years earlier. If the myth had been dispelled then, mother might have enjoyed many years of frolicking in the water with the rest of us.

I think of that story when people tell me they can't talk to employers, or to computers, or to an audience of more than five people. And I think of it when I find myself telling people that I can't do this, or I can't do that. Sure. Sure we can't. And mother can't swim.

After Thought

Mother was 86 and going strong when this was written. Need I say that she loved everything I wrote? She passed on three years later never really believing, however, that she had floated and swam to rescue Grandma.

"It was your father who saved us," she would say. "We just beat on the water until he fished us out."

Maybe. Maybe she didn't know much about swimming, but she knew plenty about living. As a young girl she worked in New York when it was a grand city offering a bowl of soup and a piece of bread for lunch for a nickle. She sold furs for Macy's and became their first telephone operator, then went on her honeymoon to California in a Model T Ford. Her formal education ended in the fifth grade, but she introduced me - even after I had graduated from college - to books and authors whom I still revere. And she more than held her own in discussing them with me.

And she knew how to die, too. After six months of feeling "not up to par," Dad got her to the doctor, who said that it looked like cancer, and that he would schedule exploratory surgery the next day. She said no, thank you, went home, stretched out on her bed, held father's hand, and went to sleep for the last time.

Way to go, Mother dear...

Welcome Back, Downtown

Welcome back, Downtown. Let's see: When were you here last? Was it in the fifties? Many of us came downtown to shop, but there wasn't much else to do. A few good movie theaters; lunch at Babe's or Younker's Tea Room, or Wolf's, or Bishop's, and that was about it.

Then you went away and took all the theaters with you, including KRNT. Many good shops went along, and Wolf's and Bishop's. Only the Tea Room and Babe's remained proud links with the past.

But now you're back, and, for me, your timing was perfect. After taking a 17-year break to work in an Ankeny cornfield-turned-college campus, I now work and live in your very heart.

At daybreak I leave my condo for the morning air, a little exercise and the daily paper. Across the street, the well-manicured grass of Nollen Plaza is a reminder of the yard where I lived on 55th Street, as are the trees that grace that block and both sides of Walnut. The air is surprisingly clean and quiet. I look in at the people taking breakfast in the Kirkwood. It seems to be the same bunch every day, and they're a happy lot.

I stand looking at an empty rack, wondering what happened to the morning paper. A car approaches and a young man jumps out with an armload. "Sorry I'm late! Here, have one on me," he says as he deftly loads the rack, folds a paper and gives it to me.

I protest, but he smiles, waves and is gone. I feel good. Welcome Back, Downtown.

I have coffee on my balcony. The city is stirring now. They're loading fruit and vegetable trucks below me at Sbrocco's as they have done for years. Cars drift silently into parking lots.

Moments later, on the skywalk, the city is fully awake and in high gear. A young woman offers a cheery "Good morning, Don!" I stand an inch taller. Welcome Back, Downtown.

Walking home on Walnut, I'm stopped by a shriveled-up old man. "Would you help me cross the street?" he pleads.

I look at him, only slightly suspicious. The odors that rise from him are not from alcohol. Let us say that he and Dial have not been formally introduced. I offer an arm and take his shopping bag.

"Thirty years brakeman on the B&O. Leg crushed between two box cars," he explains. "Hobble halfway across the street and it changes to red."

"Where do you live?" I ask.

He points to a grand old building which -- like him -- has seen better days. But it's staging a comeback. Maybe he will, too. I wish him well. I'd love to hear about the B&O, but a friend is coming for dinner.

With a pot roast on "low," we bike along the river to Douglas Avenue and back. What other city offers such a wonderful bike path?

After dinner we sip wine on the balcony. The globed street lights on Court and Walnut cast a warm and friendly glow. The streets are alive with people, and there is a line waiting in front of JukeBox. A muffled cheer comes from Sec Taylor Stadium: somebody hit a home run. The incongruous sounds of a horse's hoofs precede the sight of a carriage attended by a young man in a high silk hat. His fare is two lovers. They round the corner below us, look up at us and wave. We wave back. I can think of no place I'd rather be than here.

Welcome Back, Downtown!

After Thought

This was the only subject I was ever assigned among 50 articles over a four-year stint with the SKYWALKER. The Chamber of Commerce was pushing the revitalization of downtown and the paper devoted an issue to the issue.

I spent childhood in a small town, attended college in a small Iowa town - Pella - and enjoyed some twenty years of married life in various single-family dwellings with three children and large yards filled with plants, trees and a dog.

I mention this only to give you a feel for the culture shock that hit me when, separated and later divorced, I eventually moved into a tenth floor, one bedroom condo in the middle of downtown Des Moines. My only contact with nature was one lonely potted plant. Oh, I did, briefly, have Charlotte as a roommate - you'll read about her soon - but she didn't do much to take the sting out of single living in the heart of the city.

Luckily, new and old friends helped me adjust quickly, and I soon came to feel as much at home in an elevator as I had in a tree house.

Still, I'm glad the paper's assignment didn't come until I'd had a year to get used to it.

Fear

Betty Lou crouched low in her chair, both hands desperately grasping the hard wooden seat. The creamy complexion of a healthy 23-year-old turned to paste, eyes glazed with fear sunk deep in their sockets, knees assumed the fetal position.

"Please...no. I can't do it. Please don't ask me." Her airless voice barely escaped her drawn and trembling lips. "Some other time, perhaps..."

"But, Betty Lou," I cooed in my most soothing voice, "all I ask is one or two minutes. You'll feel good when it's over."

"No, I've thought about it all week," she whispered. "I couldn't eat before I came up here tonight. I just can't bring myself to do it. I thought it would be, well, different from this."

"But, Betty Lou," I implored, knowing that tonight was not the night, but making one final, desperate try. "A simple two-minute speech on any subject you choose. The rest of the class will support you. They all have their speeches prepared. Haven't you, Bob? Sally? George?"

This is the first presentation for my college speech class or private workshop, and early on we confront our biggest obstacle -- fear. Betty Lou is real, you know. Oh, I was playing with you a bit, but the physical and mental distress I pictured holds for men and women of every age, income level, education and national origin.

Fear of public speaking is a model for non-discrimination.

The Book of Lists includes a survey of 3,500 Americans who were asked to name their fears. Not only did public speaking lead the list, but it far out-distanced fear of heights in second place. Bugs and insects ran a distant third, followed by financial insecurity. Fear of death ranks seventh, cautioning me that it would not be wise to offer students a choice between giving a speech or facing a firing squad.

The symptoms exhibited by the hapless Betty Lou are far from unusual or extreme. When I ask students if they can identify with those I listed with Betty Lou, or with loss of memory, buzzing in the ears, dry throat, tight chest, churning stomach, sweaty palms, or weak knees, they usually reply, "All of the above."

Having discussed the problem with my students at Drake, Upper Iowa University, and from workshops sponsored by the State of Iowa, I offer the following reasons for this great fear. Admittedly, the reasons seem paltry in light of the intensity of the fear, but they are the best I've seen or heard.

Reason One: Fear of failure

If my speech does not come off well; if I can't precisely articulate what I mean; if I can't move the audience to action, or hold them spellbound, or double them over with laughter...well, people will look at me as a failure.

Reason Two: Fear of looking foolish

I'll probably forget what I want to say and be left standing there alone in front of everybody.

Then I'll babble incoherently and stumble off the platform. They won't laugh with me, they'll laugh at me.

Reason Three: Fear of rejection by my peers

If I don't get my facts right; if I forget something; if I get tongue-tied; if I look scared stiff...well, nobody likes a bungler.

Reason Four: Fear of the unknown

I don't know how to face all those people. How do I stand? What do I do with my hands? Where do I look? What do I say first, or last, or in between?

Reason Five: Fear of one-way communication

The whole weight of the conversation is on me. Nobody supports me, lets me know how I'm doing, or keeps me on the right track. I'm alone and must plod ahead until I die or until my five minutes is up, whichever comes first.

Reason Six: Fear of fear

When I get up to talk, my heart pounds, my knees shake, etc. My system is on red alert. I'm out of control, and I don't like that -- it adds to my fear even more.

All this makes one wonder how anyone ever stands up to say anything. But they do. Even Betty Lou will give her speech. It will be delivered in a monotone, without gestures, and will last less than a minute. But it will be a start, and she will gradually improve. To say that she will conquer all -- or even most --of her fear of speaking in a few sessions would be foolish of me. You know better. But when her self-confidence grows, she will be able to apply specific techniques to make her public speaking task less onerous.

No fear can stand the light of healthy self-confidence.

After Thought

Years ago, I taught a class to prepare adults in the General Educational Development (GED) program. They would sit still for the English, reading and social studies, but they would squirm in their seats at the mention of math. Fear robbed them of their ability to think.

"What is it about math that turns you off?" I asked.

"Algerba!" they sang in chorus.

"Okay. Here's the deal," I bargained. "Hang in with me through fractions, percent and a touch of geometry and we'll forget the Algebra. You'll have all the math you need to pass the test. Will you do it?"

Yes, they would do it. And they did up to the point when I would say, "This idea of equality that we're talking about works for a six pack, or a bolt of silk, so let's call the thing 'X'."

"Hold it, Don. Are we into Algebra?"

"No, no, no," I lied through my teeth. "This is just something you'll be able to use to solve many practical problems in life, as well as answer questions in the GED."

Fear of public speaking and of math is a tricky thing. You have to be tricky to get the better of it, but it can be done.

The Seven % Non-Solution

It's curious, but in the process of communicating our thoughts and feelings, the words we use account for as little as seven percent of the message others receive. The most credit I've heard words given is 35 percent, but most people who study such things put it nearer to seven.

If this is true, you may well ask what makes up the 93 percent of the message? And if it is true, why do we spend so much time and energy worrying about words and devote so little time to the 93 percent? And if it is true, then surely it applies only to oral communication, because words are all we have when we write, right?

One question at a time, please! At the rate of one column every two weeks we'll see the Ides of March before all this is sorted out. But if we begin with the second question -- the one about words being all there is to writing -- I think we can get a good start on the 93 percent. Perhaps we will see that in communication, as in arithmetic, diets, and love affairs, it is the small details which usually cause the whole thing to collapse.

Suppose we took a draft of an article such as this, typed on a machine like my ancient Royal, written on cheap yellow paper, with several words crossed out and others penciled in, and we tacked it up on the bulletin board at Clancy's

Bar.   Across the top we write "Please note!"
How many customers do you think would note?

Now suppose we take the same article, let the
Skywalker print it, and have a company
president tack it on his bulletin board with the
same "Please note!" scrawled across the top.
Might some of his employees -- the same who
are wont to slake their thirst at Clancy's -- now
plumb our article for its full meaning?   The
difference is nonverbal.

Suppose a college freshman submitted a
paper to the Skywalker called "The Power of
Words in International Relations."   Would the
Skywalker run it, and on the off-chance that
they did, would many of us read it?   But let the
freshman admit that his uncle, U. S. Senator
Blatt, sent him the only copy of a paper written
by the Secretary of State.   Now might the
Skywalker run it on page one, and might we
devour every word?

One final suppose: Suppose I worked late
into the night on this article and called you at
midnight for your reaction to it before taking it
to the Skywalker tomorrow morning.   Based
upon your reaction might I abandon any vision
of being a writer and turn to tending bar at
Clancy's?   Timing could be more of my problem
than the words I use, and timing is nonverbal.

Words, of course, are vital to every type of
communication.   But words come to naught if
people do not read or listen.   Or, having read or
heard, they forget, or misunderstand, or disbe-
lieve, or are not moved to action by these words.
And it is the nonverbal aspect of communi-

cation that lets our words get through to our audience with the message we mean to send.

The nonverbal aspect of writing is, in part, the material the words are written with and on. If you send your lover a carbon copy of a penciled letter "To my One and Only," it's a safe bet that your words won't measure up to seven percent of the message received. Likewise, carbon or machine copies of important documents may have a chilling effect upon those who receive them.

Of course punctuation and syntax and spelling are important nonverbals and must be included in the 93 percent. But if you fret over the strict rules Miss Swoop laid upon you in high school, let me know and we'll talk about it in a future column.

Until then, perhaps we can discuss it at Clancy's.

A Market For Speech

It was one of those brilliant ideas that works its way up through idle conversations. What had been carefree banter turned slightly pedantic as Walt and I sensed that the process of sexual attraction would change radically if our idea could be fully developed and marketed.

"We can do it! We can do it in about 20 lessons for about $150 a person!" Walt was pacing around my kitchen with such force that plates rattled in the cupboard.

"Look," Walt went on, "people spend hundreds every year just on their hair. Think of the money they spend on clothes just to look attractive. And think of the time women spend polishing their nails and men spend polishing their shoes -- mostly to impress the opposite sex. Add in cosmetics and deodorants and you're talking about big money."

"Right," I threw in, showing that I can rattle dishes, too. "But when these same people open their mouths and sounds come out better made by a mouse, or a moose, or chalk on a chalkboard, we know that all their time and money invested in these things has been wasted!"

"So we'll show them how to use the voice effectively," concluded Walt. "Volume, range, tone, timbre, articulation. We'll use the same skills we use in the theater!"

So we set up shop and had a spate of clients, most of whom wanted lessons to sound like Veronica Lake or Rock Hudson after one lesson. Other projects gradually claimed our attention, but 25 years later we still have the vision -- Walt on the East Coast, and I here Iowa -- because the many uses of the voice remain a largely neglected but potentially potent factor in the art of communication and in the mysterious process of personal attraction.

Let me illustrate. When I mention volume as one way to use the voice, people sometimes object that others have no difficulty hearing them. Perhaps, but volume goes beyond loudness. Changing your volume helps hold the attention of any audience, be it one or 1,000. And lowering your voice to a near whisper will dramatize any point you wish to make. Remember the prophet who said, "A soft answer turneth away wrath."

Most of us have an effective speaking range of six notes: two below our natural note, and three above it. But many of us drone on like Johnny-one-note, only occasionally dropping our voice one note to show that we have come to the end of a thought. Listen to an interesting and dynamic speaker and notice how he or she plays the voice like a musical instrument, gliding within this range to produce a spoken song which excites and entrances us. I believe that subtle use of the voice this way helps bring out the charisma in some people.

Pitch, while we're at it, refers to our "natural note" as I noted above. It is the home note from which we move up or down. This home note tends to move up the scale slightly as we become tense or excited, in much the same way that the pitch of a violin rises as the strings become taut. We would all do well to check our pitch occasionally to see if it is unnaturally high due to stress or strain.

Most of us speak at the rate of 100-150 words per minute. Last week I sat in on part of a day-long presentation by a fellow who clipped along at about 180. Mr. Enthusiasm he was, but when I checked the group at 3 o'clock, many people appeared worn out from his constant machine gun delivery. It's great to zip along at this pace for a few minutes to catch our attention, or to cover familiar ground, or to summarize the facts of the matter, but we need to slow down to deal with complex material, or to make a special point.

Pace can be used with volume and range to create a rhythm which holds an audience in thrall. Martin Luther King was a master at this, as were Winston Churchill, Franklin Roosevelt, Virginia Dole and former Senator Harold Hughes.

And Senator Hughes has another voice quality which is important to effective speaking: timbre. Timbre comes from using one's entire body as a sounding board to amplify sounds created by the vocal chords. Good singers and speakers don't need to yell into microphones: Their words seem to be, and in fact are, created deep within their bodies. Speakers with thin voices form words in their mouths where there is nothing but teeth to resonate against; speakers with nasal voices form sounds near the top of the throat and the vibrations find their way into the nasal passages. They get some resonation, but so does a cat when you step on its tail.

Helping people to make their voice more resonant is not easy, as teaching the violin must not be easy. It's mostly a matter of understanding that the sound must start deep within the body, and that at least the head and chest must act as resonators, and that we must practice.

If we are to become effective speakers, or even one-to-one communicators, then a pleasing voice is not to be sneezed at. But don't take my word for it. The next time you're on the coast, check with Walter. You'll know him by the sound of his voice.

A Cinch By The Inch

Iowa Methodist Hospital's out-patient waiting room seemed to be an unlikely place for an actor's convention, but there they all were; friends from the Playhouse, Drama Workshop, Ingersoll Dinner Theater and Charlie's Showplace. Mary Riggs, who has graced the boards of most theaters in town, greeted me with the usual question: "What part do you have in this movie?"

"I'm one of Morris Goodman's surgeons," I answered. "But I was just hired and don't know much about Goodman, or the movie. I understand it's called 'The Miracle Man.' But who are you, and what's this all about?"

"I'm Morris' mother," Mary answered in her motherly voice, "and in the next scene, another doctor is about to explain to me and to his wife what Morris' condition is following the crash of his single-engine airplane."

Bill Kulky, a drama professor, emerged from a dressing room in his hospital garb looking so professional that I was momentarily tempted to ask him about a nagging pain in my side. But Bill was rehearsing his lines with Mary and several other actors, and what I heard then, and over the next several days, made me forget any real or imagined ills.

"Mrs. Goodman," the 'doctor' said, "in my 25 years as a surgeon I have never seen a person survive a crash like this. Your husband's neck is broken at the first and second vertebrae, and either of these breaks is almost always fatal. His diaphragm is so badly damaged that he will never breathe again without a respirator. His larynx and voice box are crushed so that he will never eat or swallow. His is totally paralyzed and his kidneys and bladder are not functioning. "I'm sorry to tell you this, but my professional opinion is that he will not survive the night."

This scene was practiced and shot many times; and I watched and wondered why Art Bauer, president of American Media in West Des Moines, would make a film about a fatal airplane crash. I had noticed a man with a very stiff neck and a somewhat restricted gait talking with Don Thompson, the director, but too many interesting things were happening to think about him, until Don caught my attention and said, "You're in the next scene in the operating room, and, oh yes, Don Bell, meet Morris Goodman."

The stiff neck turned to me, a hand with a firm grip was advanced, and an unusual but pleasant voice said, " Pleased to meet you, Don."

Des Moines is a surprising place, but I'm usually not at a loss for words. "I...uh...you... uh...you're Morris Goodman? You survived that crash?"

Morris laughed. "Don, I think you'd better read my book."

I learned much from Morris that morning, and later, I picked up a copy of "The Miracle Man" from American Media. The next day, I spent several hours with Morris on the set, and we talked about his book, his accident and his recovery. Mostly we talked about goal-setting and the power of positive thinking. I learned from Morris how by sheer determination he taught himself to breathe, to speak and to eat, and, eventually, to walk. The odds against Morris doing any of these things were staggering, and I asked him -- as he has been asked many times before -- how he managed to do it.

"Never underestimate the power of the mind," Morris answered, punctuating each word. "Our bodies aren't worth much from the neck down: maybe a hundred dollars. But what we have from the neck up is priceless.

"People say that we use one-tenth of our brain power, but I don't think we use one-thousandth of it."

Morris said that we can do almost anything with our mind if we would give it a chance, but that most of us give up too soon.

"If your goal is to roll a boulder up a hill," he continued, "then it does no good to get it almost to the top. If it rolls back down you will have spent your energy and it may be further away than when you started."

Morris talked about what it takes to reach a goal. First we must understand our own strengths and needs; then set a goal that we believe we can reach rather than one other people say is appropriate for us; then build a step-by-step plan to reach the goal; then direct our total thought and energy toward reaching it.

"But," Morris cautioned, "you will never reach your goals if you associate with negative-thinking people. I avoid them at all cost."

Morris said he thought that most people had too many goals, and that he would rather set one goal and devote his entire energy to reaching it.

"How could you possibly psych yourself up to reach the almost impossible goals you set for yourself?" I asked.

Morris looked at me and said, "Don, let me give you a trite saying which has been, never-the-less, very meaningful to me. The saying is this: 'It's hard by the yard; it's a cinch by the inch.'"

I think of Morris Goodman every time I check my list of personal goals; and the goals seem much easier to reach than they were several months ago. You might want to get a copy of "The Miracle Man." After you have experienced it, you may join me in thinking that, compared to Morris Goodman, our goals are really a "cinch by the inch."

After Thoughts

Morris is well beyond moving by inches. My movie-making experience with him took place six years before this update and he now moves yards at a time. I recently talked with him at his home in Virginia Beach about his new album on goal setting and about a national TV show that he plans to produce. What a person!

The Stuff Of Life

I have a small house on Carpenter Avenue, in the very heart of the "inner city," where I spend my time when not speaking or consulting. I enjoy being there.

The neighbors in every direction are interesting. I easily mistook the mother of the family next door to be the sister of her teen-age son. He is a well-mannered young man, tall with a graceful military bearing. Like too many young black men, he finds employment hard to come by. There is a pleasant young lady whom I take to be a daughter; there is a lad of about 10, whose bike I have fixed on occasion; and there is Nakisha.

Nakisha is everything you could ask for in a 6-year-old girl. She is brimful of life, inquisitive, playful, uninhibited, trusting, funny and creative. She brings me precious gifts, and Valentines in July. She comes with paper and asks me to print her name and mine, and she looks at me, and at the writing, with wonder.

Her questions, of course, are without end:

"What is this?"

"Do you like me?"

"How does this work?"

"Do you think I'm a nice person?" she asks. She has just had a knock-down fight with her brother, and her ebony cheeks are still damp with tears. Her self-worth is in question, and she needs to be affirmed and nurtured.

I want to gather her in my arms and carry her around the yard as I did so many times with my own children. They would cling to me, and I to them, sometimes all four of us, our arms and legs so entwined that we would sink, laughing, to the ground. The nourishment we drew from that bonding cannot be found in meat and potatoes, or in a store full of vitamin pills. It is the very stuff of life, and we all thrive on it.

But Nakisha and I may never share that experience. It's not seemly for men to gather young ladies of any age in their arms and hug them.

Nakisha may not now understand, but she will soon enough, and with that understanding will come reticence. Her playful nature will turn serious. If not inhibited, she will at least become distrustful.

As she grows older, society will teach her to say "Excuse me" if she accidentally touches a stranger. When she sits in an open cafe with a young man, they will have no physical contact. Her counterparts in Italy will touch, caress, hug or squeeze 30 times in a half-hour, and couples in France will make physical contact about 20 times. In this country the couples don't even hold or touch each other on the dance floor! And which country, do you suppose, has more people crying out, often in socially unacceptable ways, for love and attention?

So Nakisha and I will be good friends. I will try to help her develop her creativity and her sense of wonder. I'd like to be remembered as someone who helped her keep zest for life alive.

Meanwhile, will you please -- alive and in person -- reach out and touch someone!

After Thoughts

I haven't been to the house on Carpenter very often in the past two years, and never at times that found the neighbors at home. Several months ago Nakisha arrived from school at the same time I did. I think I saw a little smile with a slight raising and inward thrust of her shoulders as becomes young girls when they are happy. Her "Hello, Mr.Bell, " was polite, but only that. What did I expect after two years? "Will you print my name?" From an eight year old?

No, Nakisha and I have had our moment together and the age of innocence is past. The barriers are going up. Not the barriers of hate that we saw a few generations ago, or even barriers of distrust. Just barriers that seem to be a part of our social fabric.

But the half smile and the shoulders told me that Nakisha also remembered. Our moment has not passed without leaving its mark.

"Will you print my name? Do you like me? Am I a nice person?"

Yes, Nakisha. All of the above.

Power Of The Eyes

John Donne wrote that "No man is an Island, entire unto himself. . . ," yet I find it more than sad that most of us think of ourselves as islands rarely in contact with the millions of other islands that exist near us.

You may recall that I recently commented on our seeming inability to hold, or touch, or have any physical contact with others, regardless of their sex. At a party, I was delighted when an attractive young lady asked me to dance -- until I found out that her idea of dancing was to stand two feet away from me, close her eyes and sway back and forth in time with the music.

In my book that is not dancing, nor is another pastime at dances when people line up in rows like we did in high school gym class to go through some rather complicated routines in time to music. Good exercise it is; social dancing it is not.

If we can't establish contact by touch, how can we? Eye contact is no substitute, but may be the next best thing, just as it is an essential complement to touch.

In every class or workshop I conduct on speaking or communicating, I stress the importance of establishing real, deep eye contact with people in the audience. Only to the extent that speakers do so will real communication be established. Only then will ideas, feelings and emotions bridge the channel that separates one island from another.

How powerful is eye contact? Observe two boxers, or contestants in any sport, or poker players deciding whether to bet or fold. None looks at the hands of the opponents, but at the eyes.

Does your lover love you?

Is a business associate leveling with you?

Is a young child sick or upset?

The eyes tell it all, and the eyes let you feed back your love, your sincerity and your caring.

Is eye contact powerful? Try to get your dentist or dental hygienist to look you in the eye when he or she gets close to you. Same with your barber or cosmetologist, or a good sales clerk adjusting a blouse, suit coat or neck wear. All of the above may work within several inches of your face, but they all will step back almost three feet to look you in the eye while talking. If they don't, you may be offended or upset.

Is eye contact essential to good communication? Confrontation with an officer with ticket book in hand is never easy, but looking up at one with silver-coated goggles is downright scary.

Have you shaken hands with someone who did not look you in the eye? I bet it sent you a message that a thousand words could not wash out. On the positive side, a meaningful glance across a crowded room says more than a thousand words and is latent with possibilities.

I still opt for touch and eye contact. Communication with the eyes can build bridges from our little islands to turn oceans of loneliness, misunderstanding, hate, fear and frustration into causeways for exciting relationships of friendship, love and under-standing.

The eyes have it.

Our Computer's A Little Down

I've about had it with computers. My own personal computer has decided not to let me read back most of the files I've entrusted it with. It leaves me with the terse comment "NE ERROR. OK" Well, Hal, it may be OK with you, but it's more than a little inconvenient for me. However, ol' buddy, I had been warned of your fickle ways and I took the precaution of printing out everything I told you, so all is not lost. Life goes on.

And that brings me to a thought that haunts me: Computers seem to dominate our business and personal worlds, and when one turns recalcitrant, everything grinds to a halt. How many times have you heard, "I'm sorry, our computer is down and I can't get you that information..." And you and I probably said yes, that is too bad, and perhaps, when it gets to feeling up, it will deign to answer the question.

Why can't the PERSON find the answer? Somebody put the information into the computer, and one would think it might still be available somewhere. I understand that it might be hard to find, and it might take longer to retrieve, but hard times call for hard solutions.

Last month I had a shot at an overseas workshop, and, needing a passport, I called New Jersey for a copy of my birth certificate.

"Oh, I'm so sorry, Mr. Bell," cooed the operator, "we just had the worst snowstorm of the season and our computer is down. Perhaps if you call back tamarra..."

Can you imagine that? A computer wakes up, looks out the window at two feet of snow and says "I/O error. No files available today until somebody shovels the walks."

Can't a human being take over? Every scrap of necessary information was at hand: my full name, my mother's married and maiden names, the attending physician's name, the date and hour of birth, the name of the hospital and its address. If a coddled computer could find a picture of the certificate on microfilm in a few microseconds, might not a person reel through that film in 10 minutes? And wouldn't that time be better spent reeling than sitting around waiting for the computer to get its bits together?

Oh, I know. This week I'll get calls from computer people telling me that the world doesn't work that way. My answer to them will be this: If we have stopped communicating with each other and must communicate via computer, it is high time we looked at our priorities. If we are dependent upon a computer to serve each other and to answer all our questions, then the cold and impersonal world of George Orwell is closing in.

Let's you and I talk, and inform each other, and entertain each other, and console each other. Let the computer shovel the walks.

Let Us Serve Us

Last month in this space I suggested that computers ought to be relegated to their proper place in the scheme of things. Apparently I touched a nerve, because several of you have cheered me on with "Right on, Don. The computer was meant to serve us, not us it."

Well, yes. I'm all for that, thank you. But my real clarion call is for US to start serving us. Ron Zempke, Co-author of "Service America," was in town and I had dinner with him -- along with some 70 members of the American Society for Training and Development. I was fortunate enough to sit across the table from him and pick his brain. Ron has gathered the stats and the stories to show that there is a direct and powerful correlation between service to customers and success in business -- and between a disdain for service and business failure. My own experiences -- and yours, I am sure -- will bear him out.

Recently I put on a seminar for the Iowa Retail Hardware Association. The topic I spoke on was "Sales and Service, the Inseparable Duo." The association secretary told me that hardware stores in Iowa are folding at the rate of two a week. Yes, that's two a week, and they were interested in anything that might help stop the bleeding.

A week later I dashed into a local hardware store after work looking for a fan belt for a furnace blower. (The owner had not been at the IHA seminar.) The belt they had was not quite right, but I bought it against the possibility that other stores would soon be closing and my tenants would freeze to death that very night. I asked if I could return it if I didn't use it.

"Keep your receipt," he admonished.

I found exactly the right belt at a service station, so two weeks later, proud that I had saved the postage-stamp-size receipt, I presented the belt for a refund.

"Aha! You've had this for more than a week," says the clerk. "Sorry, but noooo refund."

"Huh?" I ask, in my most articulate, communicative style.

"That's our policy," he says cheerfully, and he points to a sign on the wall that says as much.

"But," I protest, "it's just been lying in the back seat of my car...."

"Sorry," he says with finality. "That's always been our policy: nooo refund after seven days....."

I figure I spend about $200 a year in that store. They just lost a potential $1,000 over the next five years for a lousy five bucks, yet they will soon wonder why they are one of the two stores that closed some week.

Please don't get me wrong. I realize that most of the stores that close are forced into it for economic reasons beyond their control. And most store owners -- like the old fellow who used to own this one -- are service-oriented.

But businessmen like this young man are bringing on their doomsday far ahead of schedule.

But listen! If you're in need of a fan belt, I just happen to have, in the back seat of my car...

After Thought

The belt has been moved from car to the wall of my garage where it hangs as a silent reminder of poor service.

As I mentioned before, I do not need to invent stories because they abound. You will believe me, then, when I report that the hardware store mentioned above went belly up. It has been torn down and a Casey's General Store was built on the spot.

Casey's, being there to serve us, is doing well.

Groan Or Smile?

I won't admit to actually groaning as I walked from the company parking lot to my office, but whatever sounds came from me were not happy ones. Just thinking of the rejections I had faced the day before was almost enough to send me back home to bed, or at least to the employment office. One of my best clients had called to postpone a public speaking workshop until later this spring. "We'll give you a call," my contact had said.

A second call to an association I've been courting for months produced an outright rejection: "Sorry, Don, but we decided on a speaker from New York. Maybe next time...." And so the day had dragged on, with calls of like ilk.

So why should today be any better? Maybe I should have stayed in teaching. The thought caused me to laugh in spite of myself, and Oscar, the guard at the building's entrance, caught the laugh as I swung past him.

"Well, good morning to you, Don Bell," he sang out in his always cheery voice. "With a laugh and a smile like that I just know something good is going to happen to you today."

"Oscar, you just might be right," I answered, coming out of my funk. With a laugh and a smile and a good attitude -- why should I fail?

Now I'm not going to tell you that I bounded into my office and lined up speeches with Xerox, Coca Cola, and the National Chamber of Commerce, but Oscar had nudged a black cloud from overhead and the day went better than expected.

If Harvey had been on the door, I might have gone home.

Harvey was part owner of a music store I worked in to pay college expenses, and a more negative man I've yet to meet. Every day, as I walked into the store, he would tell me why we weren't going to sell anything: Monday was the beginning of the week, and Friday was the end, and nobody could be expected to buy music on either of those days. The same could be said for Wednesday, and on Tuesday and Thursday it was too hot, too cold, or too close to Wednesday.

And Harvey was right, you know. People didn't seem to want to buy music or pianos from us on any of those days.

Oh, I know that I've said that other people can't make us mad, or happy, or enthusiastic. We are the masters of our own fate, but it sure helps to have a few people like Oscar to encourage us. And what possible good can come from fellows like Harvey?

Who knows, if Oscar owned the music store, I might still be selling pianos.

Your New Seville

The goals we reach for never seem to let themselves be caught as quickly as most of us would like. The habits we try to break stick with us tenaciously; the treasures and the recognition we yearn for continue to elude us; the physical and mental toughness we sweat and strain for come by degrees almost too small to measure.

And yet, as you know, goals -- even some that seem to lie beyond our grasp -- are reached every day by people just like you and me. And most will look back upon these insurmountable goals and wonder what made them think they would be so hard to reach.

We all need the electric charge that comes from occasionally reaching a goal, or seeing someone else reach one. I've been hit by a thousand volts twice in this past month, and hearing about these two events may charge you up, or give your hair a curl or two.

The first is not as spectacular as the second, but please don't skip ahead as it is a fine example of the "sleeper effect," which tells us something about patience.

I have been working with a giant international company teaching some management people how to teach almost everyone in the company a new system the company has just adopted. The first few sessions went well, but in the fourth we got hung up on a communication technique that I asked them to try.

"Hey," they said, "that may work for you, but it will never work for us."

"Maybe not," I countered, "but if you try it you may like it."

I left with their "NO WAY!" ringing in my ears. And so it was that during my next several sessions they would come around to that point and, almost as a chorus, give me "NO WAY!"

I left them alone for a month, as planned, and when I went back last week one of their members stammered, "Don, we never would believe it, but we tried it, and we like it."

The "sleeper effect" says that none of us changes attitudes or behaviors quickly or easily. We usually have to sleep on it many nights before we come around. Be patient with yourself, and with others.

And so it is that jolt #2 came when a training director entered my office last week with hand extended. "You'll be happy to hear that George has his new white Cadillac Seville."

I was indeed. George had been in a goal-setting workshop I had conducted for the company and we had worked hard to get from the goal of "a new car" to a Cadillac, then to a Seville, and finally to white. I asked him to cut out a picture of that exact model and post it where he would see it several times each day. In addition, he was to write the description on a card and read it several times a day. He gave me a half-hearted "Sure" which I took to mean "So much for that Mickey Mouse idea, Bell."

The training director tells me that George continued to "think about it" until he heard that another class member achieved a small but impressive goal in slightly more than a month. Then he found the picture, cut it out, and got down to serious business on his goal. And now he has his white Seville.

Most of us give up much too quickly. We write off our interactions with people as being non-productive, and only a few failures convince us that we can't alter our own destiny.

Try it. Continue to try. There are white Sevilles rolling off the line every day, and a year from now one of them could be yours.

After Thought

This piece says much the same thing as the one about Morris Goodman, <u>A Cinch By the Inch.</u>

Perhaps I need only one in this little book.

Perhaps two says something about my feelings on goal setting.

Our Only Competition

It was break time for my college class, and Tim approached with a sheepish grin. "I talked with a friend who, apparently, is no friend of yours," he said.

"Ouch," I grimaced, "I'm sure I have my share of those, but who is this one, and what's the problem?"

"Lady named Jane Doe. She's a public speaker, like you," Tim offered.

"Doe? Jane Doe?" I pondered. "Can't place the name. Did I say something deleterious to her character?"

"I think you landed a speaking engagement that was deleterious to her pocketbook."

"Is she saying that I bribed a meeting planner or tapped her phone, because I assure you..."

"No, no, no," Tim quickly protested. "It's just that she sees you as her enemy: her competition. And you know how some people feel about competition. She took umbrage that I, her trusted friend, would stoop to taking a class you taught."

"Tim, I'm sorry she sees it that way," I replied, comforted that I had not, in an unguarded moment, cast aspersions upon Ms. Doe's ancestry.

"I have only one really mean competitor,

and he has nothing to do with Ms. Doe. In fact, I'd like to meet Jane. Perhaps we can do each other some good: share engagements that don't fit our particular talents or schedule. But my real competitor would never work with me like that."

"And who is this terror of the speaking circuit you so dread?" asked Tim, playing to the small circle that had gathered. "Does he under-bid you?"

"Bidding doesn't bother me," I said. "It's fair to assume that most people who bid less than I do give less. And I may give less than those who bid $5,000. No, my competitor is much more devious. And he takes more work from me than I'll ever lose through the bidding process."

He seemed curious, so I pressed on. "A while back I was writing an article and he said, 'Better watch the World Series. This could be the last game.'

"I protested, but soon found myself glued to the TV. After the game I went back to my word processor, but he would have none of it. 'Too late to think creatively,' he said. 'Get a good night's sleep and hit it hard in the morning.'

"And in the morning he was there with an-other great idea: 'Why not eat out? Your break-fasts are kind of drab...'

"I almost fell for it, but quickly fixed a bacon and cheese omelet, just to show who's boss.

"Later, at the office, there he was, perched on the edge of my desk, full of advice: 'No need to proof that; Don't bother to log that appointment - you'll remember; Why spend time on that bid? They've never given you any business; Forget the research; you can wing it.'

"On the way home he took another tack. 'Better go dancing tonight. You can work on your book later.' He knew he had me and he laughed with glee.

"Tim," I sighed, "If Jane carries around a competitor half as fierce as mine, she has absolutely nothing to fear from me. See if she'll meet me for lunch."

After Thought

I write these articles to let you know what I've been thinking, and when I wrote this three years ago I was thinking quite often about my running battle with this fellow inside my head.

I'm not singing 'poor little me,' but you understand that it's not easy going from 18 years with a government agency - a community college - where they put the same nice pay check in your hand every two weeks, to waking up unemployed every morning. Nobody put a check in my hand then until I delivered a speech or a workshop. Sometimes the checks were fat, sometimes they were thin and sometimes it was a long time between checks. You can imagine what the "competitor" was saying, and that the least damning but most persistent little gem was "Get a job: a real job. One that puts a check in your hand every two weeks."

And three years have not stilled his voice. Yes, the checks are fatter now, and they come more frequently, but that fellow still whispers in my ear "But what about *next* month?"

And what about the one person in a hundred who tells me she is disappointed with my presentation? My competitor forgets the 99 who gush about how great it was: He zeros in on the one and says "Get a real job."

Do I win my battles with him? Sure. Remember, I teach positive thinking and the power of constructive self-talk. I win the battles, *but the war goes on.*

We are, all of us, fragile beings and we all have a voice that rages within us. The voice only wants to protect us from change, because change faces us with the unknown.

We win our battles by constantly talking to the voice. It's probably not a good idea to talk to it out loud *in public,* but our days are full of opportunities to remind it that we're okay; we welcome change; and we're in charge.

Hard Work Makes It Easy

" A million dollars, Don," she said, "I'm going to make a million dollars."

"Great," I replied, "Please remember my special projects that need funding. But first, how do you plan to make this million?"

My friend had invited me for morning coffee with the promise of exciting news. "Well, Don," she instructed me patiently, "If it's to be, it's up to me!"

I waited, in vain, for more. "If what's to be, Sally?" I finally asked.

"I have this concept about health," she began, picking up speed, "I took pictures of a gorgeous couple leaning against a refrigerator with captions saying 'Eat Your Way to Health.' An investor wants to fund the concept."

"Good for you, Sally," I said, "But, uh, what concept? Have you worked out the details?"

She seemed vexed at my lack of perspicacity and reverted to spelling out each word. "The concept is that we can eat our way to health. Details will be worked out after funding."

I talked some about carts before horses and agreed that there are millions to be made in nutrition. I suggested that she faced hours of creative thinking to design an unique approach that would bring her the million. It was not my place to tell her what might be wrong with her idea, but to help her discover what was right with it. My comments were met with "If it's to be..." Fortunately, her investor moved the meeting to an unspecified future, thus saving her a long and fruitless drive to Minneapolis.

Our conversation took place months ago, and I thought of it this week while visiting my friend Milt Jacobs in San Diego. Milt, too, believes "If it's to be,..." but he knows that without a logical plan, slogans are meaningless.

Milt came here looking at semi- retirement based on income from his Iowa farmland. Like many Iowans, he watched helplessly as the value of his land sank to pre-war levels. But Milt is an entrepreneur, not a dreamer. He said "If retirement is to be, it's up to me," and started a mid-life career in the stock market.

While in San Diego, we enjoyed a gourmet dinner for single people. The women in that city are almost as attractive and interesting as those in Iowa. But at 10 o'clock, when others wanted to go dancing, Milt came home -- dragging me with him -- to face several hours of work in preparation for the market opening. And at 6:30 a.m. we were glued to the TV, not watching the "Ollie North Show," but intent upon AMEX, Jones, Puts, Calls, Straddles, Spreads. We ate breakfast with an eye on TV and an ear to a computer that spoke through a telephone.

Unconcerned with the long run, Milt observed that a price movement in either direction tends to persist for at least several hours. He located a group of mutual funds that permit him to switch every hour at low cost. Based on that concept, his investments have done extremely well. "It it's to be" is fine, but a logical plan -- backed up with hard work -- makes it all come true.

After Thought

Four years is a long time for a market strategy to survive, so you'll be interested to hear that Milt is doing as well in 1990 as he did in 1986 when I wrote this article. Many people in Southern California would be surprised to learn that every day has *two* six o'clocks, but, as I wrote then, Milt is dressed and in his bedroom/office before 6 AM.

I don't know if the voice he carries around in his head ever tells Milt to get a real job. I doubt it does because he has been an entrepreneur most of his life, but if it does, Milt has good cause to laugh at it.

It is role models like him who help me deal with the voice in my head and assure it that I don't need a "real" job with a "regular" pay check. What Milt and others like him teach us is that success come to us if we really *think*, about ways to use our particular minds and/or hands to move us toward particular goals.

Sometimes the idea of thinking scares us, because we don't consider ourselves smart enough to think of anything very brilliant.

Not to worry. When you consider that many of us have gradually allowed our thinking process to degenerate into figuring out a slate of

TV shows that will get us through the evening without thinking or talking, you realize that a little genuine thinking goes a long way.

The folks at Domino's thought that many of us would like hot pizza delivered within a half hour; Forman and Clark thought we'd walk up one flight for a wide variety of suits; Milt thought that the Market, like sheep, followed a pattern often enough that, with careful study, he could predict its behavior. Brilliant? Maybe, but the key is that these folks turned off the TV, stared out the window and thought it through. They determined that they had whatever talent and brawn it took for that line of work, then they went to work.

Right after Cheers and Wheel of Fortune, I'm going to do the same.

Care to join me?

Seeing More Clearly

On a long drive to Chicago 25 years ago, I was accompanying a friend who was to give the keynote address at a convention of some 2,500 people, and we had stopped for a break at a cafe. A waitress approached, gave me a questioning look, and I responded with "Coffee, black, please." My friend added, "Coffee will be fine."

The waitress looked at me, then at my friend, then back at me. "Does he take cream?" she asked.

As you travel the sidewalks and skywalks of Des Moines, you probably encounter more blind people than you might expect to find in a city of this size. You may have wondered about them: Should you say "hello" as you pass? Should you ask to help if one seems lost? Should you hire them if they apply for a job with you?

As you may have surmised, the gentleman with me on the Chicago trip was blind. He was, and still is, Dr. Kenneth Jernigan, former director of the Iowa Commission for the Blind and current president of the National Federation of the Blind.

The waitress was not acting out of meanness when she put the question to me. She would never admit to prejudice, only to pity. She did not know me or Dr. Jernigan, but she

73

could see that he was blind, and that was enough. How could he know what people put in the coffee they gave him? If she had ventured to ask him she might have stood about six inches from his ear and yelled the question at him. The blind are often assumed to be deaf. And they are often assumed to be stupid.

Some time after the coffee incident, I introduced a blind woman to a downtown businessman who was looking for clerical help. After the introductions and general questioning had established that the woman's ability to hear, understand, and speak English far exceeded his requirements, he threw up his hands and said to me -- not to her, but to me -- "I'd like to use her, but the job requires some typing."

"Oh, that's no problem," she replied. "I type well over 55 words per minute."

"But she'd have to answer the phone, and take messages, and things like that," he countered weakly, searching for some air-tight excuse. It was not long in coming.

"But, Mr. Bell," he said slowly, "this position is *here*, on the *fifth* floor!" He explained that all floors would seem the same to a blind person, and this woman might get off at four, or six, and create all sorts of problems. Explanations about Braille markings would not move him. Like me when I first met Dr. Jernigan, this businessman was handicapped by a lack of sensitivity and understanding. His handicap cost him a diligent and intelligent employee; mine almost cost me a good friend and mentor.

When I was introduced to Dr. Jernigan I was not prepared to confront blindness. I stammered, "It's good to see you, sir," then apologized for using the word "see" in his presence.

He took no offense and reminded me that seeing implied much more than use of the eyes; it is based in perception. That put me at ease. Later, I could ask if he had read the morning paper, knowing that if he had read it, it was through the eyes of another person, and he had probably seen things that escaped me and the person doing the reading.

Most of us get by the best we can, handicapped by our inability to analyze, or synthesize, or extrapolate, or digest carbohydrates, or work 12 hours without rest, or relate events to their causes, or make verbs agree with their subjects, or read a prospectus, or remember names, or conquer our fear of public speaking, flying or failing.

If we can accept these and hundreds of other characteristics, why balk at blindness? If you would befriend and talk with someone like me who freely admits to being encumbered by more baggage than appears on the above list, then you should also talk without pity or embarrassment to the one who is blind. If you would hire one of us based upon our qualifications, then hire the blind, who are also one of us, based upon theirs.

Incidentally, I think Dr. Jernigan will tell you that he does take cream with his coffee. And don't try to palm off one of those insipid non-dairy creamers. He'll see through it with the first sip.

After Thought

After building the Iowa Commission into what was universally recognized as the best facility for training, rehabilitation and service for the blind in the world, Dr. Jernigan moved to Baltimore to devote full time to the National Federation of the Blind.

The NFB will celebrate its victories and lay plans for the future at its 50th annual convention to be held this year in Dallas.

Kenneth Jernigan and the NFB win their battles, but the war goes on. The war goes on.

Plan Not To Fail

I had watched my neighbor's son grow through public school and on into college. Last year, as we chatted over the back fence, he spoke with pride about his coming graduation from a prestigious Eastern university.

"That's great, Tim," I said, shaking his hand. "By the way, what field did you major in?

"History," said Tim, nodding his head to affirm his point. "I'm a history major."

"History?" I was not prepared for that answer. Tim had seemed more interested in the present than in the past. "Do you plan to teach or do research?"

"Teach? Research? No, those sound kind of dull to me," he grimaced.

I asked him, "What do you plan to do with your history major?"

Tim wasn't prepared for my question.

"Well," he sputtered, "I guess I'll get a job...I'll look for a job in, probably some sort of business, maybe."

My wife called me to the phone, so the question was never fully resolved, but I thought of Tim last week while doing a workshop on goal-setting for college students and other young adults. We were talking about career goals and a vivacious young lady asked, "I'm in my first semester in word processing. What do you think of that as a career?"

I, of course, told her that my thoughts would be of little value to her in choosing her career, and I asked her what she thought about it.

"Well, I'm not sure. Just what does a word processor do?"

"You have carefully considered careers ranging from accounting through zoology and you picked one near the end of the list -- word processing -- without knowing what a word processor does?"

Her reply was more of a question than a statement: "I assume they work with people as they type..."

Having just told her that my thoughts on the subject were of little value to her, I told her my thoughts.

"A word processor sits at a highly sophisticated typewriter/computer from dawn to dusk. The main contact she or he has with people is over the headset of a dictating machine. Word processors are highly intelligent and must catch spelling and grammar errors made by people who are often paid five times what they are."

"Oh, no," she cried. "I need to be around a lot of people, and I hate to sit still for five minutes."

And five minutes is about how long she would last in word processing.

Now I'm not knocking this young lady, or word processing, or Tim, or history as a major; but I think most of us would do well to give more thought to the careers we follow. Are you inclined to work best with people, with things, or with concepts? No one of these is better than the other two, and there are countless opportunities in all three areas that are challenging, exciting, and lucrative.

The trick for each of us is to find that unique balance of exposure to people, things, and concepts that fills our need for authority, prestige, excitement, money, security, routine, service, or a dozen other factors.

If you have searched and found your balance, then you have wealth that cannot be expressed by money in the bank.

I'm grateful that I can work at what I like to do, but it has taken many years, with many false starts that might have been avoided with better planning. But it could be worse: I could be teaching the history of word processing.

Charlotte

Charlotte moved in with me last August. I came home to find her, petite and leggy, perched above my computer. My inclination was to throw her out, but, standing on a chair to observe her, my awe for her and her wondrous web overcame my territorial imperative.

How had she found her way to my tenth floor condo? Had she hitched a ride on my pants as I walked through Nollen Plaza? What reasoning process led her to set up shop by the ceiling rather than, say, between my desk and telephone: territory I would be unwilling to share with her? How did she construct a web so perfect, this creature smaller than a grain of rice? In admiration and respect I ceded to her that small corner of the room above my computer. In return she would deal with whatever flies and insects made their way to our lair. It was a good arrangement, not demanding of either party.

I sit at the computer some four feet below and contemplate how to duplicate her web. No plan comes to mind. My sophisticated computer graphics program can't touch it.

We talk about artificial intelligence - AI - and suggest that computers may be privy to a kind of thinking process that lets them make decisions without checking every possibility, and to modify their own programs without human help. A checker-playing computer does that and I read that it can now beat its creator.

Fine. I'm a student of artificial intelligence, but I'm also a student of a universal intelligence we begin to see at work in Charlotte's web.

She looks down at me and seems to say, "Am I and my web not wonderful?

"Hey! What about you, big fella?" she adds. "If I can do all this with my pin-head brain, think what you can do. Why, if I had one billionth of your brain cells I'd build me a web to catch every bug from here to Kansas City!

"Don't just sit there staring at a blank paper, you two-legged wonder: THINK! Use your abundant share of this universal intelligence!"

Thanks, Charlotte. I needed that. Let's see if I have this...

"Charlotte moved in with me last August. I came home to find her, petite and leggy..."

How Do *You* See You?

I didn't know what to expect when I knocked on Bob's door. Twenty-five years can do strange things to people.

I was in his city doing a workshop on communication skills, and called from my hotel on the chance that we still had common interests.

Bob sounded happy to hear from me and without even a "Do we have an extra steak" aside to his wife, invited me to his home for dinner.

I thought of Mark Twain's comment that he would speak to any group for $50; $100 if he had to eat at their banquet. My workshop included a banquet, and I saw no way of avoiding it, so my visit with Bob would be limited to a short half-hour.

When he answered the door, I was pleased to see that the years had gone easy on Bob. The living room he led me to showed evidence of financial security. Not a six-figure income, but more than comfortable. As we stood talking I noted that he looked young for his age, even agile as he darted about the room preparing a seat for me.

There was a pause as we settled into our seats, and I closed the gap by asking what he did for a living.

"What do I do?" he said weakly. "Why, I don't do anything. Retired, you know."

No, I didn't know.

"Worked for years wholesaling the best sporting goods around, but people don't want to buy from an old duffer like me. They want the young, good-looking kids with the new ideas. So I took my early retirement and hung it up."

"So how do you spend your time?" I asked. "Do you travel much?"

"Travel? No. I guess I've seen all there is to see and eaten everything worth eating. I stick close to home.

"Thought about jogging, but nothing is more disgusting than an old fool puffing down the sidewalk. Leave it to the young gazelles. I ride an exercise bike in my room."

"But, Bob," I protested, "you're not that old. What are you, late 50's, early 60's?"

"Not old!" he shot back, avoiding a direct answer. "You call this sagging body 'not old'? Nobody even cares about me anymore. Kids left home long ago, and they never call. Friends have drifted off. You're the only person to show an interest in me for a long time, but what made you call?"

It seemed like a strange question to ask, so it was not easy to answer. "We worked together; were friends; shared interests. "

The conversation shifted to people we had known and things we had done years ago. We worked through the ritual and I took my leave, promising to keep in touch. We won't, of course. The distance is too great, and there is nothing to keep in touch about.

I've written before about self-concept, suggesting that it determines who we are: how much money we make; how much good health we enjoy; what sort of people we surround ourselves with and what we think of them, and really, what they think of our self.

I've tried to make the case that our self-concept determines for us what we can do and what we cannot do.

But my recent experiences with Bob show a darker side of our self-concept that we might want to look at very carefully. Bob demonstrates that our self-concept tells us when to "hang it up," give it over to other people, sit back and wait for the end to come.

One day soon Bob will pass away after going nowhere on his stationary bike for 25 minutes. He might just as well go run in the Boston Marathon and live to be 100, but his self-concept won't let him.

Whether you are 20 years older than Bob or 40 years younger, it is still the way you see yourself that makes you decide that you are too old or too young. And it is often because the world sees people of our age as being senile or immature that we build this negative view of ourselves. This same self-view, however, can let you know that you are now in your peak years, that people will walk through fire to deal with a person like you.

Colonel Sanders' self-concept was working well the day he bought a fried chicken business from a fellow whose self-concept told him that he had no future selling greasy chicken.

The colonel was in his 70's, and that turned out to a good age for selling chicken that was finger-lickin' good.

I hope your self-concept tells you that there are exotic places to visit and revisit, delicious new foods for you to eat and exciting new things for you to do.

Doing nothing more than riding an exercise bike in your bedroom might be dangerous. It could bore you to death.

After Thought

Two years later and Bob hangs in. I called him to bring this article up to date for you, and he sounded fine. I know it would make a good story if I could tell you he has come upon hard times, but I'm not that short of material, and I'm not trying to moralize in any event, and I'm happy to hear that he's doing well.

I must say that he found it hard to believe that my wife and I are going to New York next week on a theater tour.

"New York?" he gasped. "You couldn't drag me there."

I didn't argue with him, but yes, New York. It's the Big Apple and we'll bite into it. Then comes Kansas City, Baltimore and Dallas.

It keeps us young. I feel like I'm in my thirties.

I like that.

My wife likes it, too.

Something Or Nothing

"**D**on't look now," I whispered to my dinner companion, "but who is that fellow at the corner table?" Jacqui, of course, immediately looked, shrugged, and disclaimed any knowledge of the gentleman.

We were enjoying a fine meal at Noah's and I felt -- as you may have felt upon seeing a face from the past -- that I had known this person more than casually.

"We've taught in the same college, or worked together, or served on a committee, or shared a jail cell, or something," I said, trying to work it out. Jacqui reminded me that I've never been inside a jail cell, and while that reduced the possibilities by one, it was scant help.

The man soon walked by our table and I introduced myself, saying that I had trouble recalling his name. He said that he was John Naylors, and that my face was familiar but our past relationship escaped him for the moment.

We took turns mentioning possibilities, but nothing came close to a fit and the best we could do was to say that it was good to see each other again.

Why do we forget some names and remember others? I suspect I've been in John's presence longer than the three hours I spent with Willard McMillan, but you notice that I remember Willard. I sat next to him on a flight to New

York and we fell into an easy conversation, as strangers often do. He was at least thirty years my senior, and I asked him what kind of work he had done as a young man. The question seemed to surprise and intrigue him. "As a young man?" he questioned. "Well, as a young man I signed on with a railroad crew breaking ground out West."

I got the impression that it had been an experience unlike anything his colleagues back East would expect of him. I pressed for details and learned about laying railroad ties, Mexican laborers, desperados, sand storms, and tarantulas. He was interesting, and he was interested in me.

Did I know that Bell and McMillan were members of the same Scot clan? Where and when had my part of the clan settled in this country? Was there a common thread that our careers or our lives had followed? He asked no question without a purpose, took careful note of each answer, fixing me in some special niche in his memory. I'll bet he remembers my name, as I remember his.

Why do we forget some names, or at least relegate them to some obscure corner of our memory? Probably because we never got really interested in the person attached to the name. Chances are that when we were introduced we worried more about making a good impression than about the person or the name. Later we were embarrassed to ask for it again, and cleverly carried on conversations without having to use a proper name.

The person remained an amorphous "you": "It's good to see you; how have you been?" We ask, "What do you think?" rather than "What do you think, Nancy?" and we are more concerned about our upcoming response to Nancy than in Nancy as a person, or in what Nancy might have to say. It's not so much that we later forget Nancy as it is that we don't have anything to remember.

Apparently John and I never asked those questions of each other that really mattered, and we never listened to the answers. Perhaps we sat across a table at some monthly board meeting and never talked to each other except about items on the agenda.

Too bad. He looked like an interesting fellow.

Anything I Can Do?

Recently I spent several days in a local hospital and had ample time to observe the quality of service. Service, after all, is the one thing that separates one hospital from another, as it separates one supermarket, or insurance company, or gas station from all others.

My purpose here is not to review the service at this particular hospital as Freda Nahas might review a play, but to use the experience to point out how good service can do wonders for your spirit, and the want of it can leave you dispirited.

Nothing epitomizes service more than a pleasant nurse. How they manage in the face of constant crisis is beyond my ken, yet I have rarely seen one give in to the pressure. Perhaps the faint of heart are quickly weeded out, leaving only those who are really concerned for the comfort and well-being of their patients. And so it was at this hospital with the nurses and the medical staff. My resident surgeon had a bit of M*A*S*H's Hawkeye in him, especially Hawkeye's ability to relate to his patients.

On the down side, there passed through the ward a slow but constant stream of people with clipboards or note cards who represented some service organization or some department of the hospital. It was their task - or so it seemed to me - to contact every person on their list. Many, but not all, by any measure, seemed to focus on the *contact*: They had too much to do to worry about service. Most of these people were volunteers, and you might say that I have no right to come down on them. Maybe. A hospital cannot function without dedicated volunteers, but if you volunteer to be of service, then merely making contact can do more harm than good.

A chaplain enters our room. "Mr. Green? Mr. Green, I'm Chaplain Blue. How are you today?"

"I'm fine, Chaplain, thank you..."

"You're fine. That's good. O.K. Anything I can do?" He checks his list and quickly moves to the next bed.

"Mr. White? Mr. White, I'm Chaplain Blue. How are you today?"

"Pretty good, I guess..."

"Pretty good. That's good. O.K. Anything I can do?" (Check)

He moves on to Mr. Brown with the same patter. (Check)

He approaches my bed and I'm tempted to answer his stock question with, "Poorly: I'm bleeding from both ears," to see if that, too, will bring "Bleeding from both ears. That's good. O.K. Anything I can do?" (Check). Instead I make it easy with the almost obligatory "Fine."

He looks not at me or my roommates. He does check the headboard to be sure the name matches his card. He hurries across the hall to make his four contacts there.

I feel for him. He is missing the joy, yes, the exhilaration that comes from real service, and I'll bet you a pack of 3x5 cards that he is as tired at night as the nurse who has worked ten times as hard, but who knows that she has made a difference.

He was a nice looking fellow and not unpleasant. Perhaps he found, as many of us have, that if you give most people in a hospital bed an inch to tell you how they are, you get back a mile of gory detail. Or perhaps he had just lost a tough one and at that moment, being human, he didn't much care how we were.

But, even then, Hawkeye would care. Perhaps all of us might reflect occasionally on what makes our being here important. I think we'll find that meaningful concern - call it service - is a lot more than "How are you? Anything I can do?" Check.

After Thought

You will not be surprised to hear that this piece brought me a phone call from the volunteer coordinator at the hospital. She was upset; her volunteers were upset; the Chaplain thought I was unfair.

I'm sorry. The focus of all my workshops on communication skills, sales and service and getting along with people, is to help people understand and use their strengths, not to dwell on their weaknesses, but I went the other way here. If I had it to do over, I'd at least leave out the name of the hospital as I've done in this rewrite.

To make amends, I put on a free two-hour seminar on service for the volunteer staff. Several were a bit hostile going in, but I think we were all friends at the end of the session.

When I went in for a final check-up Hawkeye and the nurses seemed extra nice.

Sky Dive, Anyone?

Have you ever been asked to do something -- make a speech, teach a class, dance the Moon Walk, sky dive from 5,000 feet -- and demurred only because you thought you didn't know enough about it? You are not alone.

During the 10 years that I tried to entice people into teaching adult education classes, the leading excuse for passing up the opportunity -- and it led by 10 lengths -- was, "I'd love to, but I don't know enough about it."

A woman called, saying, "You won't remember me, Mr. Bell. I was in a creative writing class you talked to last year and I said I would think about teaching a class in Indian lore."

"But I do remember you," I protested. "You sat in the back of the room; you are tall, dark, and good looking." It is not that I have a fantastic memory; she was the first and only person to suggest a class built around American Indians, and I was impressed.

"Well, yes, thank you," she admitted. "I've been thinking about it for a year, and I may be ready. But I'm not sure that I have enough information to teach for 10 evenings. Could you possibly come to my home to look over my material?"

That very evening my wife and I drove to her home. It was easy to find: she had a huge totem pole in the front yard, and once inside we felt we had gone back 300 years. Almost every item from rugs to cookware was American Indian-related. Her walls were lined with hand-made booklets cataloging the history of more than 1,000 Indian tribes.

And yet it took the full persuasive powers of my wife and me to convince this charming and intelligent woman that she indeed had more than she needed to handle an adult education class. I suggested that she really had more than enough for a semester-long graduate seminar. Finally, we got through to her.

It will come as no shock to you that the 18 people who signed up for her class -- several of whom were well versed in Indian lore -- were delighted. All but three stayed on for Indian Lore II, and would have signed on for Advanced Lore III had she not repeated the first class due to the heavy demand.

I could tell you the equal to this story 10 times over. I might write of a married couple who finally took on teaching a gourmet cooking class, then pestered me with the unfounded fear that I wouldn't let them teach it again. I could tell of a person who, despite 30 years in the business, was terrified that questions would be asked about antiques that she couldn't answer.

Of course such questions were asked, and for each question there was a different student who was proud to answer from his or her field of special interest. The teacher found, to her relief, that it was not expected of her that she know all the answers.

The world's expectations of us are not nearly as great as we believe them to be. If we speak or teach, the world asks that we have a good grasp of our subject; that we know how to find the answers to questions about unfamiliar material; and that vanity does not compel us to pass out misinformation to hide our deficiencies.

If you've never talked, written or taught something that is of interest to you, give it a try. Take a shot at the Moon Walk. People don't really care if you look foolish: they have their own dances to worry about. Why not skydive? There is only a little to learn about it, and the rest is faith.

And I'll teach, and talk, and write, and learn, and dance along with you. But I may not sky dive. I never said that my faith is without limits.

After Thought

Stress! Yes, stress is a major reason why we don't sky dive or give a speech. I think that once we realize that the stress is in *us*, rather than in the *activity*, we can begin to see where - and how - we can deal with it.

I had lunch with a rancher during a seminar in Montana. "I can't begin to see how you do this, Don," he said. " I'm stressed out just being in a room with twenty people like this, let alone talking to them."

"Being in a room with twenty people causes you stress," I repeated. "I wonder why? You run a ranch bigger than New York City; you use good English; you're clean and good looking. What do you do to relax?

"There's a deep crater with a clear pool on the top of a hill on my ranch," he said, and I could tell by his eyes that he wished he were there. "I put on SCUBA gear and go down about ten feet, then through a passage into a dark cavern. It's quiet there. Not another living thing, and I relax."

"Relax!" I shuddered. "You take me down there and I'll claw a hole through the roof quicker than a ground squirrel. Joe, now we're talking stress!"

But where is the stress? Is it in the cavern, or in me? Is it in the roomful of people, or in Joe? Once we take responsibility for the stress, I think we can talk to ourselves and get a handle on it. It's not easy, but it's better than blaming the cavern or the people.

Who Are These Strangers?

Drop in on any management seminar or after-dinner speech and chances are good someone will be talking about change. You'll hear that technology changes at breathtaking speed, leaving us hard put to cope. You will be told that the bomb is changing our view of war and AIDS our view of sex.

While many of us talk about changes in people, and how to bring them about, rarely does anyone note the rapid change *of* people: where Tom worked yesterday, Dick or Harriet works today. Where corn grew yesterday, a mini-town sprouts today.

I thought of this last week when I hied off to the Community Playhouse to catch their fine production of "Anything Goes." Being alone, I spent my time people-watching. As I stood by the door watching the crowd file in, it came as a bit of a shock that out of 440 people I could call fewer than a dozen by name, plus a dozen or so I knew vaguely.

Many years ago, when I acted some at the Playhouse, I suppose I might have named at least 100 people at any performance. I still attend, but not being active, I have not cultivated that particular theater crowd.

So, who were all those strangers? I might as well have been in Tallahassee. What became of all the people I once knew?

Well, many have left Des Moines for other jobs, or other climes. Some have passed on, and some have just passed on theater, giving themselves over to video cassettes. For whatever reason, they have been replaced by others who will stay awhile, then themselves move on.

While this may be unsettling and discouraging at times, it is also good news if you have relationships that grow tedious, or if your sales are off. Need to break out of a slump or a rut and meet new people? Does a certain buyer pass you over in favor of his brother-in-law? Is your competitor (if you believe in the win/lose concept) an aggressive workaholic? Don't worry. Change will work in your favor.

Bruce Barton, former dean of American ad men, spoke eloquently about this, using the biblical Joseph as an example. You recall the story: Joseph had a beautiful coat of many colors; he was betrayed by his jealous brothers, carried off to Egypt and sold into slavery. He worked his way into the king's favor by interpreting dreams, and rose in authority over all of Egypt second only to the king. Yet, the Book of Exodus says, years later when the king passed away, the new king 'knew not Joseph'. Imagine that. Joseph has dominion over all the land, and goes into semi-retirement for a few years and a new-age king doesn't even know him.

Continue to advertise and to tell your story, admonishes Barton, because there is a new crop of folks coming up who never heard of you or your product.

Small wonder I recognized anyone at the Playhouse after 25 years. I haven't kept pace with change in that area. But there are hundreds of new people out there that both you and I can meet and enjoy and sell to and entertain and be entertained by. We just have to be open to change.

So cheer up! There are exciting days ahead. And it's a safe bet that next time you call on that dead-end account, the new buyer won't have a brother-in-law waiting to steal your business.

Strangers in A Strange Land

Rachel and David showed up at my wife's adult basic education class looking for help with their English. They explained, in somewhat halting but understandable terms, that they were Russians newly arrived in this country.

Conversational English, or English as a Second Language, is not the focus of that class, but Jacki is an easy mark for people who sincerely want to learn. She put Rachel to work on a basic English test to get a feel for her comprehension of our language, and asked David to try a little math test. Both agreed and repaired to a small desk to consider their assignment.

They were up almost at once. Rachel gave her paper to Jacki; David handed his to me.

It was your basic math test: How much is 27 divided by seven; if bananas are 27 cents a pound, how much is one banana, or some such thing. It revealed quite a bit about David, however. Because he took only a short time to complete it, I figured that he had not done well. I looked at the neatly printed answers and found what you may have guessed: He answered every question correctly.

David looked slightly embarrassed as he said, "In Russia I am Engineer. I have 300 peoples work for me design roads and bridge." So much for your basic math test.

And so it was with Rachel. She went through the English test like Daniel Webster and sheepishly revealed that she had been an elementary school teacher in Russia.

We became good friends with this charming young couple and their two delightful children. They came from Kiev to escape persecution as Jews, and had joined a small contingent of their countrymen who preceded them to Des Moines. They came to our house for Thanksgiving dinner and it was with great pride that we explained the meaning of this holiday. The parallels between their recent trip and that of the early pilgrims were not lost on any of us.

The holidays are a time for sharing, and you might consider, if you have not already done so, inviting a stranger or two for dinner. Perhaps you know an older couple who has no kin nearby, or a family down on their luck, or strangers in our land. Open up and invite them in. My guess is that you'll all have a great time, and that the increased understanding you all gain will make you feel better about our world and the people in it.

After Thought

Their names are not "Rachel and David," but other than that - as in all these articles - the facts are the facts.

Rachel and David moved to Chicago, and my former wife and I corresponded with them for some time. We're lucky to have them in our country. For one thing, our "roads and bridge" need all the help they can get.

Beyond War

It was a new experience for me, standing on the skywalk over Seventh Street with Carol Reinhard, collecting signatures for a peace movement. I have spent a lifetime talking with people, teaching and being taught, entertaining and being entertained, persuading and being persuaded, but never have I done these things on the run.

It is more than slightly unnerving to fall in stride with strangers who are hurrying to lunch on a busy skywalk, hoping to gain their attention and interest in something less than the distance between the Marriott Hotel and Bankers Trust. If the cause had not been a good one, I would have pleaded an important luncheon engagement for myself and left the task to braver souls.

But the cause is good, for the Beyond War Foundation has set the worldwide goal of bringing the people of all nations to realize that all war - not just nuclear war - is obsolete.

At first blush it looks like an easy task, for who can be in favor of war? But new modes of thinking are not easy for any of us, and objections are raised about our "enemies" desire for peace.

The foundation makes an award every year to an individual, group or nation who makes a significant contribution toward building a world without war. In 1983, the award was given to the National Conference of Catholic Bishops;

and last year the recipient was the International Physicians for the Prevention of Nuclear War, a unique group of 105,000 physicians from 54 countries. This year it is to be given to the presidents and prime ministers of six countries who issued the Five Continent Peace Initiative in January of this year.

So it was that this upcoming award had many of us on the skywalk and around town last week collecting signatures of support for these six world leaders. The foundation hopes to collect one million signatures to present, via satellite, on December 14, in an historic presentation.

North America, South America, Europe, Africa and Asia will be linked for the first time by live television, and the award and the signatures will be presented to Raul Alfonsin, president of Argentina; Rajiv Gandhi, prime minister of India; Miguel de la Madrid, president of Mexico; Julius Nyerere, president of the United Republic of Tanzania; Olof Palme, prime minister of Sweden; and Andreas Papandreous, prime minister of Greece.

Isn't that exciting - five continents linked by television for peace? I hope to see you there, but if you can't come at this late date, let me wish for you peace, and Happy Holidays.

After Thoughts

This, of course, was written in 1985, and the ceremony lived up to its billing. Since then, Olof Palme has been assassinated and the world has seen many changes.

It is encouraging to note that the foundation has been able to expand its focus. They still talk about the East/West war and they have added North/South, which is the war of the poor and the rich nations; the Outer War with the environment; and the Inner War we are waging against drug abuse.

We win the battles. The war goes on, but we're making progress. We're making progress.

Love And War

When my two boys were very young they liked to fight, as most kids do. Nothing serious, you understand, as brothers can't do much damage to each other when one is six and the other is three. They would flail away, and cry, and shout and cry some more, out of frustration more than pain.

Each, in his turn, would come to me or his mother with protestations about being the innocent party. It was always, "He started it. I didn't do nothin'."

"Anything," I would say. "I didn't do anything." It is hard to reason with the immature, but it is never too soon to start on rules of grammar.

Having made my point, I quickly moved away from English usage and warfare. "If you young tigers can cool it, your sister might join us for a dish of ice cream while I read us the latest story by Dr. Seuss."

It always worked. Ice cream, entertainment and togetherness win out over fighting every time with the young.

That is not to say that differences were nevermore resolved with fists. One boy was placed on an advanced track in a different school and that brought taunts of "We're number one!" with the automatic response, "Oh, no you're not: We are!" Blood was sometimes let to resolve that weighty issue, with righteous cries of "I can't let him get away with that, Dad. I had to teach him a lesson."

The lure of ice cream and a story became less effective, and both young men worked on building their bodies, the better to defend themselves. What was once a harmless roundhouse swing was now a punishing uppercut.

I am thankful that with physical maturity came maturity of character. They could reason now, and I sat them down, not to ice cream and Dr. Seuss, but to a discussion about the consequences of their actions. They had fought for years and nothing had been permanently resolved. No great damage had been done, but energies had been spent that might have been used to better advantage, and now each was strong enough to do irreparable damage to teeth, eyes, kidneys or other vital organs, the functions of which were not yet apparent to them.

I pointed out that our house seemed to be growing smaller, and that we were a family unit in which a hurt to one was felt by us all.

I talked about blood, and said that their mother and I, whose blood was not at all alike, loved each other; that we loved each of our three children, and they loved us, as their blood was a mixture of hers and mine. "But you three share blood that is more alike than any other. How much then," I asked, "should you love each other?"

That made sense to them. That, plus a large dose of maturity. Today they are as closely knit as three people can be, and I am intensely proud.

But I don't tell you all this because I am proud of my children. I tell you because I have just been watching the evening news.

After Thoughts

All three children flew back from homes in California to be at our recent wedding. No fights, jealousy or tension. Teja played classical guitar at the ceremony (His <u>Dolphin</u> <u>Smiles</u> has been in the top three new-age albums) ; Dave shared ring-bearing with Jane's Liz (Dave is a very successful building contractor on the Coast; Liz does very well at The Principal); and Victoria lit the candles with Jane's Julie (Victoria has been awarded the top service award from her company four years running; Julie is a Freshman in college).

Jane and I are blessed.

Don Bell
Management Management, Inc.
2413 - 81 Circle • Des Moines, Iowa 50322
515 253-0834